"Bring the Classics to Life"

TREASURE ISLAND

LEVEL 2

Series Designer
Philip J. Solimene

Editor
Kathryn L. Brennan

EDCON

Long Island, New York

Story Adaptor
Nikki Berkowitz

Author
Robert Louis Stevenson

About the Author

Robert Louis Balfour Stevenson was born on November 13, 1850 in Scotland. He did so well in school that at sixteen years old he entered a university. His parents wanted him to study law. But, he wanted to be a writer. Even though he was ill all his life, Robert Louis Stevenson became a famous writer. Some other children's stories written by him are: The Strange Case of Dr. Jekyll and Mr. Hyde, Kidnapped, and Prince Otto. Robert Louis Stevenson died on December 3, 1894 at the age of forty-four.

Copyright © 1995
A/V Concepts Corp.
Long Island, New York

Printed in U.S.A.
ISBN# 1-55576-050-3

CONTENTS

Words Used 4, 5

WORDS USED

Story 31	Story 32	Story 33	Story 34	Story 35
KEY WORDS				
ago	answered	angry	ahead	climb
leg	eyes	careful	believe	cried
sea	myself	exciting	clever	fight
stories	quiet	remember	join	roar
terrible	shook	secret	kill	taken
watch	wild	wonder	might	through
NECESSARY WORDS				
blind		crutch	bush	beach
cutlass			enjoy	knife
dead			fever	safely
fifteen			nineteen	
rum			pirate	
			spot	

WORDS USED

Story 36	Story 37	Story 38	Story 39	Story 40
KEY WORDS				
cut	bottom	corner	count	even
quickly	cap	piece	mean	joke
rope	hardly	short	only	mind
round	hit	shut	sign	shovels
strange	sure	small	still	suddenly
until	throw	swish	whispered	together
NECESSARY WORDS				
chance		sand	Bible	raised
cool			fever	
tip				

THE CAPTAIN'S STORY

PREPARATION

Key Words

ago	(ə gō´)	in the past *This took place long ago.*
leg	(leg)	one of the parts of the body you use to walk or stand on *He broke his leg playing ball.*
sea	(sē)	a large body of water *We sailed across the sea.*
stories	(stôr´ ēs)	reports that tell about something *He told many stories about horses.*
terrible	(ter´ ə bəl)	very bad *She was a terrible person.*
watch	(woch)	to look at for a long time *We kept watch for the tall man.*

THE CAPTAIN'S STORY

Necessary Words

blind	(blīnd)	unable to see; having no sight
		The blind man had a seeing-eye dog with him.
dead	(ded)	no longer alive
		My pet "Buttons" has been dead for five years now.
fifteen	(fif tēn´)	the number after 14
		I will be fifteen years old next week.

People

Black Dog   a man with two of his fingers missing. He is looking for the captain.

Captain Bill   a tall, heavy man with a cut across one cheek. His real name is Billy Bones.

Dr. Livesay   a friend of the Hawkins family; a doctor and a man of the law.

Flint   a mean pirate that buried the treasure that Jim Hawkins and others are looking for

Places

Admiral Benbow Inn   a house where you must pay to stay overnight and also get food and drink. The house was owned by Jim Hawkins' parents.

Treasure Island   a small body of land that is surrounded by water which is believed to have money, jewels, etc., hidden on it.

Things

Black spot   a piece of paper like a summons (ticket)

cutlass   a short, heavy knife with a curved single-edged blade

rum   a liquid drink that has alcohol in it

THE CAPTAIN'S STORY

When the captain had too much to drink, he would frighten everyone in the inn with stories about what happened on his ships.

Preview: 1. Read the name of the story.
2. Look at the picture carefully.
3. Read the sentence under the picture.
4. Read the first paragraph of the story.
5. Then answer the following question.

You learned from your preview that this story is about
___ a. life on an island.
___ b. a hidden treasure.
___ c. a strong captain.
___ d. a happy family.

Turn to the Comprehension Check on page 10 for the right answer.

Now read the story.

Read to find out about some strange things happening at the Admiral Benbow Inn.

THE CAPTAIN'S STORY

I am Jim Hawkins. Let me tell you the story of Treasure Island from beginning to end. The only thing I won't tell you is how to find this place. You see, treasure is still hidden there.

Long ago, a tall man of the sea came to stay at our Admiral Benbow Inn. Captain Bill, as we came to call him, had a deep cut across his face. He kept a large sea chest in his room. By day, he would look out over the sea and watch for a man with one leg. At night, he would drink rum. When he was drinking rum, he would tell us stories about the sea. He liked to frighten us all with terrible stories about hangings. He would sing at the top of his voice:

FIFTEEN MEN ON
A DEAD MAN'S CHEST
YO HO HO AND
A BOTTLE OF RUM.

It was during that long, cold winter that my dad became sick. My mom took care of him. I took care of the Inn. One morning, a seaman, with two fingers missing on his left hand, called to me, "Sonny, is my mate Bill here?" Before I could answer, he pushed me behind the door. Then he watched like a cat for a mouse.

At last, the captain came. As he gave the door a push, the strange man called, "Bill, it's your mate from long ago."

"Black Dog," Captain Bill said in a whisper.

A minute later, their talking became angry shouts. Bill took a swing at the man with his cutlass. He hit the sign above the Inn's door. In a flash, Black Dog ran off.

"Jim, I need rum," cried the captain, as he fell to the floor.

It was late evening when the captain woke up. I told him how Dr. Livesay had saved his life.

"Never mind," he shouted as he tried to roll on his side. "If Flint or the man with one leg finds me, I'll be given the Black Spot."

Then, right in the middle of everything, my poor sick father passed away suddenly. It wasn't until later that week that I found out the secret of the Black Spot.

I was sitting outside on a rock feeling bad about my father. A sorry man came up beside me. He couldn't see. He was blind. He asked, "Where am I Mate?"

"The Admiral Benbow Inn," I answered, as I took his hand. He quickly pushed my arm behind my back until it hurt.

"Now," he said in a terrible voice, "take me to the captain!"

As we went into the Inn, I knew it was not a happy surprise for Captain Bill.

"The time has come Bill," the clever man said, as he gave him a small piece of paper and left quickly.

Bill opened his hand and cried, "Ten o'clock!" He was so afraid that he tried to jump up and run. I heard him make a strange noise. There was nothing I could do. Then he fell to the floor, and the life went out of his body for good.

THE CAPTAIN'S STORY

COMPREHENSION CHECK

Choose the best answer.

1. Who is telling us this story?
   ___a. Admiral Benbow
   ___b. Jim Hawkins, the son of the Inn's owner
   ___c. The captain
   ___d. A man with one leg

2. Locked away in his room, the captain kept
   ___a. a tiny dog.
   ___b. fifteen men.
   ___c. a large sea chest.
   ___d. a radio.

3. By day, the captain would look out over the sea and watch for
   ___a. a man with one leg.
   ___b. rain.
   ___c. the sun to come up.
   ___d. Admiral Benbow.

4. The captain would frighten everyone with stories about
   ___a. the circus.
   ___b. the zoo.
   ___c. the Admiral Benbow.
   ___d. hangings.

5. One day, the captain took a swing with his cutlass at
   ___a. Black Dog.
   ___b. Jim.
   ___c. Jim's mom.
   ___d. Sonny.

6. The captain told Jim that if Flint or the man with one leg finds him, he will be given
   ___a. a new car.
   ___b. the Black Spot.
   ___c. a lot of money.
   ___d. another bottle of rum.

7. After the blind man gave a small piece of paper to the captain,
   ___a. the captain died.
   ___b. they shook hands.
   ___c. they sat down together.
   ___d. the captain went to get his chest.

8. The captain came to the Inn to
   ___a. find some treasure.
   ___b. hide from someone.
   ___c. eat dinner and sing.
   ___d. meet a friend.

9. Another name for this story could be
   ___a. "Great Happenings."
   ___b. "My Friend Flint."
   ___c. "A Good Feeling."
   ___d. "The Captain's Secret."

10. This story is mainly about
    ___a. Admiral Benbow.
    ___b. Jim Hawkins.
    ___c. Flint.
    ___d. Captain Bill.

Check your answers with the Comprehension Check Key on page 67.

This page may be reproduced for classroom use.

THE CAPTAIN'S STORY

VOCABULARY CHECK

ago	leg	sea	stories	terrible	watch

I. Sentences to Finish

Fill in the blank in each sentence with the correct key word from the box above.

1. We set our sails and headed for the _____ .

2. Grandfather has told us many _____ about when he was young.

3. My sister fell on the ice and broke her _____ .

4. Mom asked me to _____ my little brother while she goes out.

5. "Long _____ this land belonged to the Indians," said the teacher.

6. I had a _____ time at the dance. I will never go again.

II. Crossword Puzzle

Use the words from the box above to fill in the puzzle. Use the meanings below to help you choose the right answer.

Across

1. very bad
3. in the past
5. a large body of water

Down

2. reports that tell about something
4. you use this body part to walk
6. to look for a long time

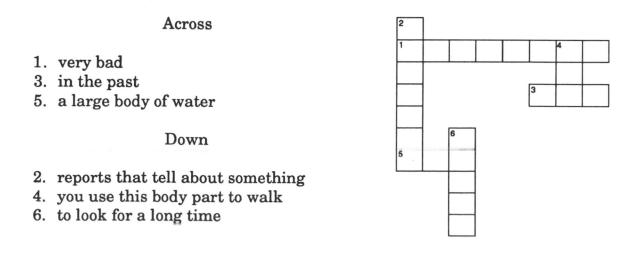

Check your answers with the key on page 69.

GETTING READY

PREPARATION

Key Words

answered	(an´ser ed)	said something when someone asked a question *"No thank you," I answered.*
eye	(ī)	the part of the body we see with *His eyes were the color blue.*
myself	(mī self´)	me *I fixed myself some breakfast.*
quiet	(kwī´ə t)	keep still, not moving *We kept quiet when mother came in.*
shook	(shu̇k)	to shake all over *I was so afraid that I shook when I saw them.* to move your hand up and down with another person *We shook hands when we met.*
wild	(wīld)	not able to stop; not in proper control or order *The wild children ran into the street.* a crazy look *He had a wild look in his eyes.*

GETTING READY

Necessary Words

People

Long John Silver   the cook on the Hispaniola (also called Barbecue)

Pew   a blind man who is looking for Silver and the map

Mr. Trelawney   a tall man with a red face. He is Dr. Livesay's friend.

GETTING READY

Mother took only enough gold to pay for what the captain owed us.
Then, as we heard others coming, we ran as fast as we could.

Preview:
1. Read the name of the story.
2. Look at the picture carefully.
3. Read the sentences under the picture.
4. Read the first paragraph of the story.
5. Then answer the following question.

You learned from your preview that Jim Hawkins and his mother
___ a.   went to a birthday party.
___ b.   ran to town to get help.
___ c.   did not get along with each other.
___ d.   sold the Inn.

Turn to the Comprehension Check on page 16 for the right answer.

Now read the story.

Read to find out what is inside the captain's locked chest.

GETTING READY

It grew dark as my mother and I ran to town. We knew we would need help later that night. After telling our story about the captain, everyone backed away. They were afraid. One man gave my mother a gun. Then he sent a young boy to tell Dr. Livesay our story. Maybe the doctor would send someone to help us.

We hurried home. I quickly locked the door. Mother's eyes were upon the captain's body. She said, "We must get the key and open the chest." There was very little time left and my hands shook when I pulled the captain's shirt open. I found the key. I cut the string around his neck, and the key fell into my hand.

Inside the chest were new clothes, broken sea shells, and two guns. Mother moved some old papers and found a small bag of gold. We were counting the money, when the quiet was broken. We heard a noise outside. It was coming closer and closer to the Inn. Mother took just enough money to pay for the captain's room. We left everything else. We hurried down the back stairs and ran.

From under the bridge, we watched. The men went wild and kicked down the door. "Find the chest," cried Pew, the blind man. We heard the sound of things breaking as they raced through the Inn. When they found the chest, someone shouted, "There is nothing left!"

"Where is that boy?" Pew shouted in a wild voice. "I should have pulled his eyes out myself."

I was so afraid that I, shook all over. My poor mother passed out.

The sound of horses racing across the bridge stopped them from finding us. They ran out the front door leaving Pew standing in the middle of the road.

"Mates," he called, "you won't leave old Pew here, will you Black Dog?"

No one answered him. I watched the blind man fall. When he stood up, he ran straight into the horses as they came across the bridge. That was the end of Pew.

I carried my mother back to the Inn. Later, when all was quiet, I rode with the men to Dr. Livesay's house.

"What were they after?" he asked. "Gold?"

"Maybe this," I answered. I reached into my sock and pulled out a paper I'd taken from the chest.

At last the doctor smiled, "It's a treasure map." The men jumped up and down and shouted at the same time.

"Give me two weeks and we'll have the best ship ever!" said Mr. Trelawney, a friend of the doctor.

We spent many days getting ready for the long trip to Treasure Island. After a long wait, Mr. Trelawney found a cook. His name was Long John Silver and he had one leg missing. (I didn't see this man until it was time for us to get on the ship.)

Finally, Dr. Livesay came for me. "Are we ready to go?" I asked.

"Tomorrow," he smiled.

"At last," I cried. I could hardly wait.

GETTING READY

COMPREHENSION CHECK

Choose the best answer.

1. Jim and his mother went back to the Inn to
   ___a. have a party.
   ___b. get the key and open the captain's locked chest.
   ___c. clean it up.
   ___d. put it up for sale.

2. All Mrs. Hawkins wanted from the chest was
   ___a. enough money to pay for the captain's room.
   ___b. the clothes.
   ___c. the two guns.
   ___d. some old pictures.

3. Jim and his mother ran from the house when they heard someone coming because
   ___a. they had to catch a train.
   ___b. they wanted to surprise them.
   ___c. the Inn was a mess.
   ___d. they knew they were in danger.

4. What happened to Pew, the blind man?
   ___a. He found what he wanted.
   ___b. He bought the Admiral Benbow Inn.
   ___c. He was run over by horses.
   ___d. He went to Dr. Livesay's house to stay.

5. Pew and his men were looking for
   ___a. Captain Flint.
   ___b. guns and horses.
   ___c. money and a map.
   ___d. food and drink.

6. Who was it that sent the men and horses to help Jim and his mother?
   ___a. Pew
   ___b. Dr. Livesay
   ___c. Black Dog
   ___d. Captain Bill

7. Dr. Livesay, Mr. Trelawney, and Jim find that the paper Jim had taken from the captain's chest was
   ___a. a treasure map.
   ___b. a bill.
   ___c. a love letter.
   ___d. a ticket.

8. The men decide to get a crew and a ship together to go find the treasure. Who turns out to be the cook on the ship?
   ___a. Jim's mother
   ___b. The man with one leg missing
   ___c. Jim.
   ___d. Dr. Livesay

9. Another name for this story could be
   ___a. "Broken Sea Shells."
   ___b. "Friends Forever."
   ___c. "From Under the Bridge."
   ___d. "The Chest."

10. This story is mainly about
    ___a. people looking for a treasure map.
    ___b. Dr. Livesay and his men.
    ___c. Jim's mother.
    ___d. Jim's father.

Check your answers with the Comprehension Key on page 67.

GETTING READY

VOCABULARY CHECK

answered	eyes	myself	quiet	shook	wild

I. Sentences to Finish

Fill in the blank in each sentence with the correct key word from the box above.

1. The sun is so bright it hurts my _____ .

2. I was all by _____ , and I was afraid.

3. The animals were running _____ in the street.

4. My teacher said I _____ all the questions right.

5. I was so cold, that my whole body _____ .

6. In any library you must be _____ .

II. Word Use

Put a check next to YES if the sentence makes sense. Put a check next to NO if the sentence does not make sense.

1. I use my <u>eyes</u> to hear with.   ___ YES   ___ NO

2. If I am all by <u>myself</u>, I am alone.   ___ YES   ___ NO

3. We <u>shook</u> hands when we met.   ___ YES   ___ NO

4. There was so much noise, that it was <u>quiet</u>.   ___ YES   ___ NO

5. My sister <u>answered</u> the telephone.   ___ YES   ___ NO

6. Father told us to sit still and be <u>wild</u>.   ___ YES   ___ NO

Check your answers with the key on page 69.

SETTING SAIL

PREPARATION

Key Words

angry   (ang´grē)   feeling mad
> *He made me angry when he called me names.*

careful   (ker´fəl)   giving lots of thought before doing something
> *I was very careful to check the water before I dove in.*

exciting   (ek sīt´ing)   having strong feelings about something
> *It was exciting to see the dancing bears.*

remember   (ri mem´bər)   thinking about something again; not to forget
> *I remember when I won the prize.*

secret   (sē´krit)   keeping something you know to yourself
> *I kept the secret for a long time.*

wonder   (wun´dər)   want to know about
> *She will wonder if I'm coming.*

SETTING SAIL

Necessary Words

crutch   (krŭch)   a stick or support used to help someone walk
Grandfather uses a <u>crutch</u> to walk.

Places

Hispaniola   the ship Dr. Livesay bought to help find the treasure

Spy Glass Inn   an inn near the docks

SETTING SAIL

At first, Jim began to wonder about Long John Silver. Silver was a clever man.

Preview:	1. Read the name of the story.
	2. Look at the picture carefully.
	3. Read the sentences under the picture.
	4. Read the first paragraph of the story.
	5. Then answer the following question.

You learned from your preview
___ a. Long John Silver liked to skate.
___ b. Long John Silver and Jim were best friends.
___ c. Jim had to give a letter to Long John Silver.
___ d. Jim did not like ships.

Turn to the Comprehension Check on page 22 for the right answer.

Now read the story.

Read to find out what kind of man Long John Silver is.

SETTING SAIL

After breakfast, the doctor gave me a letter. I was to take the letter to Long John Silver. It was exciting to see all the ships as I walked past the Spy Glass Inn. I can still remember Silver standing near the door. He had one leg missing. He used a crutch to help himself walk around.

"Mr. Silver?" I asked, as I handed him the letter.

He smiled and said, "So, you're the cabin boy." He was about to shake my hand. Suddenly, a man beside me stood up. As he placed his drink on the table, I saw he had two fingers missing.

"Black Dog," I shouted, when he ran out the door.

"Black who?" Silver asked. In an angry voice, he then said, "Never mind, he didn't pay me for his drink. After him, mates."

While the men chased him, I told Long John Silver the exciting story about the captain and the Admiral Benbow Inn.

"Oh yes, I have seen him before. As I remember, he used to come in with a blind man," said Silver.

"That was Pew," I said.

"You're quick lad," he answered.

I was beginning to wonder about Silver but he was too clever for me. He kept me busy as we walked to the ship, with stories about the sea. He never found Black Dog.

When we stepped onto the Hispaniola, we heard the ship's captain shouting. He was angry that Mr. Trelawney had picked the men to work on the ship. He said there would be trouble. Someone had told the secret about the treasure. Dr. Livesay was a careful man. We put all the guns in one place. If anyone tried to take over the ship, they would have to think of another way.

Life on the Hispaniola wasn't all bad. The days were filled with hard work. At night, the men would tell stories and sing:

FIFTEEN MEN ON A
DEAD MAN'S CHEST
YO HO HO AND A
BOTTLE OF RUM.

For a minute, I felt like I was back at the Inn listening to the Captain.

One day when my work was finished, I went to the large wooden box that was filled with apples. There were two left in the bottom. I climbed in. I was about to fall asleep, when I heard Silver's voice.

"Ah, I lost my leg the same time Pew lost his eyes," said Silver. "We were part of Flint's ship."

"We could frighten the likes out of anyone," said another man.

Silver talked to his men. "This trip we'll be careful to take it slow. When we get to the island, we'll do them in. Until then, every man keep quiet and keep our plans secret. To luck and to Old Flint."

I began to wonder what would happen to us. The next sound I heard was the man on the lookout shouting, "Land Ho!"

SETTING SAIL

COMPREHENSION CHECK

Choose the best answer.

1. When Jim met Long John Silver at the Spy Glass Inn, he also saw
    ___a. a cabin boy.
    ___b. Black Dog.
    ___c. Admiral Benbow.
    ___d. the captain.

2. Long John Silver told Jim that Black Dog used to come to the Inn with
    ___a. the blind man, Pew.
    ___b. his father.
    ___c. his mother.
    ___d. the captain.

3. Silver's men chased Black Dog, but
    ___a. they didn't find him.
    ___b. Black Dog gave up.
    ___c. Jim told them not to.
    ___d. Jim found him.

4. When Silver realized Jim was starting to wonder about him,
    ___a. he hit Jim over the head.
    ___b. he started to cry.
    ___c. he ran away.
    ___d. he kept him busy with stories about the sea.

5. The captain of the Hispaniola was angry because
    ___a. the ship wasn't big enough.
    ___b. Mr. Trelawney had picked the men to work on the ship.
    ___c. there wasn't enough food on the ship.
    ___d. he wanted to tell everyone about the treasure.

6. When Dr. Livesay found that someone had told the secret about the treasure,
    ___a. he just laughed.
    ___b. he was angry because he wanted to tell everyone.
    ___c. he put all the guns in one place.
    ___d. he said he wasn't going on the ship.

7. When Jim was in the wooden box where no one could see him, he heard Silver and his men
    ___a. planning to take over the ship.
    ___b. singing a happy song.
    ___c. planning a surprise party for him.
    ___d. talking about how much they liked the quiet of the sea.

8. Long John Silver wanted Jim to think he was
    ___a. kind and gentle.
    ___b. loud and wild.
    ___c. old and tired.
    ___d. big and tall.

9. Another name for this story could be
    ___a. "The Spy Glass Inn."
    ___b. "Long John Silver."
    ___c. "Hard Work."
    ___d. "The Chase."

10. This story is mainly about
    ___a. getting a ship ready for sea.
    ___b. delivering a letter.
    ___c. Jim finding out about Silver's plans.
    ___d. a large wooden box filled with apples.

Check your answers with the Comprehension Check Key on page 67.

SETTING SAIL

VOCABULARY CHECK

angry	careful	exciting	remember	secret	wonder

I. Sentences to Finish

Fill in the blank in each sentence with the correct word from the box above.

1. If you tell me a _____ , I give you my word I will not tell anyone.

2. We had an _____ day at the zoo.

3. As we went out the door, Mom shouted, "Please be _____ !"

4. John is _____ with me because I did not wait for him.

5. I told my teacher that I would _____ to bring in the signed note.

6. I _____ what is inside this box.

II. Matching

Write the letter of the correct meaning from Column B next to the key word in Column A.

Column A

1. secret   _____

2. remember   _____

3. wonder   _____

4. careful   _____

5. exciting   _____

6. angry   _____

Column B

a. feeling mad

b. having strong feelings about something

c. keep something you know to yourself

d. think about something again

e. want to know about

f. giving lots of thought before doing something

Check your answers with the key on page 69.

TROUBLE ON THE SHIP

PREPARATION

Key Words

ahead	(ə hed´)	in front of
		They were in the line <u>ahead</u> of me.
believe	(bi lēv´)	to think that something is true
		I <u>believe</u> we were the oldest people there.
clever	(klev´ər)	being smart and quick
		He was very <u>clever</u> and won the game every time.
join	(join)	to become part of the group
		Please <u>join</u> our club.
kill	(kil)	to put an end to
		The cat wanted to <u>kill</u> the bird.
might	(mīt)	maybe
		My father <u>might</u> take me to the game.

TROUBLE ON THE SHIP

Necessary Words

bush/bushes   (bŏŏsh/bŏŏsh´es)   low branching plant(s) that are smaller than trees
The little rabbit was hiding in the <u>bushes</u>.

enjoy/enjoying   (ĕn joi´/ĕn joi´ing)   to get pleasure from; to make happy
I hope you <u>enjoy</u> yourself at the party.

fever   (fē´vər)   a higher than normal body temperature
I stayed home today because I had a <u>fever</u>.

nineteen   (nīn tēn´)   one number after 18
If I am eighteen years old now, on my next birthday, I will be <u>nineteen</u>.

spot   (spŏt)   a specific or certain place; a mark on a surface
"Where did this <u>spot</u> on the floor come from?" asked Mother.

People

Captain Smollet   is the man who is the captain of the Hispaniola.

pirate   one who robs the land from the sea

Places

Skeleton Island   an island where all the pirates are put to rest

TROUBLE ON THE SHIP

Long John Silver tells the captain and others what he knows about the land they have spotted.

Preview:
1. Read the name of the story.
2. Look at the picture carefully.
3. Read the sentence under the picture.
4. Read the first three paragraphs of the story.
5. Then answer the following question.

You learned from your preview that the land they spotted
___ a. was safe.
___ b. had houses built on it.
___ c. had been hit by a storm.
___ d. had pirates on it at one time.

Turn to the Comprehension Check on page 28 for the right answer.

Now read the story.

Read to find out what happened on Treasure Island.

TROUBLE ON THE SHIP

The seamen ran from everywhere to look at the island.

"Has anyone ever seen that land ahead?" asked our ship's captain.

"I have," said Silver. "Over there is the lookout called the Spy Glass. Skeleton Island is there. That's where all the pirates are put to rest."

"Thank you," said our captain. "You can go now. We might need you later."

I wanted to run and tell Dr. Livesay the terrible things I had heard. Silver came walking over to me, so I had to wait.

"This is a great spot for a young boy," he said. "You can go swimming and hunting. Why, I feel like I have my ten toes again. I'll pack you some food when you're ready to go."

It was hard to believe he could say this after what I'd heard.

"What is it lad?" asked Dr. Livesay as we came together. The doctor, the ship's captain, and Mr. Trelawney were surprised to hear that Silver planned to kill us.

"What a very clever man he was to have tricked us all," said Dr. Livesay.

There was nothing left to do but to go on to the island. We had only six men. They had nineteen, but we believed we were safe until we found the treasure. The closer we came, the more I began to hate Treasure Island. The wind had stopped. We sat rocking on the water. The air felt heavy.

We were all hot and tired. The men began to fight with each other. Dr. Livesay smelled the air and said, "I don't know about treasure, but I'll bet there is fever here." Captain Smollett called a secret meeting. He gave each one of us a gun. We made our plans and then joined the others. I was afraid Silver and his mates might take the ship over at any minute. The captain must have felt that way, too. He said, "Men, you can go to the island for the afternoon." He let Silver take charge. That way, they would not guess we knew their plan to kill us.

"Jim," Silver called as we landed on the island. But I ran ahead of everyone so I could look around by myself. I was enjoying the island, when I heard two voices coming closer. I hid in the bushes. I listened.

"You're a fine lad," Silver began. "I wanted to tell you of our plans before anything happened. Will you join us Mate?"

Suddenly, there was a loud cry from the other side of the island.

"What was that?" the lad asked.

"Someone who wouldn't join us," laughed Silver.

"I wouldn't join the likes of you men." He turned to walk away. Silver knocked him down with his crutch. Then he pulled out his cutlass and killed him.

I could not believe what I saw. I ran as fast as my legs could carry me. How could I go back to the ship? But that wasn't the end of it. There was something else that made me stop short in my tracks.

TROUBLE ON THE SHIP

COMPREHENSION CHECK

Choose the best answer.

1. Just as Jim was about to tell Dr. Livesay the terrible things he had heard,
   ___a. he fell off the ship.
   ___b. Dr. Livesay said he didn't want to hear it.
   ___c. Silver hit him on the head.
   ___d. Silver came walking over to him.

2. Silver told Jim that the island was a great place to go
   ___a. hunting and swimming.
   ___b. looking for pirates.
   ___c. looking for treasure.
   ___d. sailing.

3. When Jim told Dr. Livesay that Silver and his men were going to try to kill them and take over the ship, Dr. Livesay
   ___a. said Silver would never do that.
   ___b. said that Silver was a clever man and had tricked them.
   ___c. didn't believe Jim.
   ___d. threw Silver off the ship.

4. Even though Jim and his men were smaller in number than Silver and his men, Dr. Livesay felt they were safe
   ___a. because Silver was really a good man.
   ___b. because Jim was a good fighter.
   ___c. until the wind stopped.
   ___d. until they found the treasure.

5. At the secret meeting Captain Smollett called, he gave Jim and his men
   ___a. a ticket home.
   ___b. a gun.
   ___c. a flag.
   ___d. a telephone.

6. When the captain let the men go to the island, he let Silver take charge
   ___a. so they would not guess the captain knew about their plan.
   ___b. so Silver would not be angry.
   ___c. because they liked Silver.
   ___d. because no one else wanted to take charge.

7. When the man told Silver he would not join him and his men,
   ___a. Silver said it was all right.
   ___b. Silver cried and kicked his feet.
   ___c. Silver killed him with his cutlass.
   ___d. Silver ran as fast as he could.

8. Silver acted nice to Jim because
   ___a. he liked Jim.
   ___b. he wanted Jim to believe everything he told him.
   ___c. he was afraid of Jim.
   ___d. Silver was a very nice man.

9. Another name for this story could be
   ___a. "The Secret."
   ___b. "The Fever."
   ___c. "The Sea."
   ___d. "A Great Island."

10. This story is mainly about
    ___a. swimming and hunting.
    ___b. how happy everyone was on the ship.
    ___c. the danger that Jim and his men were in.
    ___d. what good friends all the men became.

Check your answers with the Comprehension Check Key on page 67.

This page may be reproduced for classroom use.

TROUBLE ON THE SHIP

VOCABULARY CHECK

ahead	believe	clever	join	kill	might

I. Sentences to Finish

Fill in the blank in each sentence with the correct key word from the box above.

1. Please come and _____ us.

2. Mom said that I _____ be able to go with you.

3. I was _____ of you on line.

4. That cat was going to catch the mouse and _____ it.

5. The teacher told me I was very _____ for my age.

6. It is hard to _____ that story she told.

II. Word Search

All the words from the box above are hidden in the puzzle below. They may be written from left to right or up and down. As you find each word, put a circle around it. One word, that is not a key word, has been done for you.

W	B	N	J	O	I	N	A
J	E	Z	X	Q	B	C	H
K	L	N	R	T	D	F	E
I	I	M	I	G	H	T	A
L	E	V	R	O	M	S	D
L	V	C	L	E	V	E	R
P	E	K	T	U	W	X	Z
O	Q	S	A	P	P	L	E

Check your answers with the key on page 70.

THE SURPRISE

PREPARATION

Key Words

climb	(klīm)	to go up higher
		I can <u>climb</u> to the top of the hill.
cried	(crīd)	to shout out
		"Help," he <u>cried</u> out to us.
fight	(fīt)	hurting another person(s) until someone wins
		We had a <u>fight</u> because he pushed me.
roar	(rôr)	to talk loud
		"Come here," he said with a <u>roar</u>.
taken	(tāk´n)	took over
		She had <u>taken</u> my car when I wasn't looking.
through	(thrü)	from one side to the other
		I walked <u>through</u> the woods before dark.

THE SURPRISE

Necessary Words

beach   (bēch)   the sand, rocks, or pebbles along a body of water
In the summer, my family likes to go to the *beach*.

knife   (nīf)   an instrument with a handle and a sharp blade used for cutting
Always use care when cutting with a knife.

safely   (sāf ly)   to act in a safe manner; free from danger or harm
The airplane landed safely.

People

Ben Gunn   one of Captain Flint's crew. He was stranded on Treasure Island for three years.

THE SURPRISE

What was it that Jim saw? A bear, a man, or a monkey?

Preview: 1. Read the name of the story.
   2. Look at the picture carefully.
   3. Read the sentences under the picture.
   4. Read the first paragraph of the story.
   5. Then answer the following question.

You learned from your preview that
___ a. Jim was still on the ship.
___ b. Jim saw something in the trees.
___ c. Jim liked to run.
___ d. Jim was never afraid.

Turn to the Comprehension Check on page 34 for the right answer.

Now read the story.

Read to find out what Jim finds on the island.

THE SURPRISE

Something moved quickly before me. I had nowhere to run. Maybe I should climb a tree. Because I was more afraid of Silver than this thing, I called, "Who are you?"

"Ben Gunn," the man whispered, as he stepped from behind the tree. He fell to the ground and asked, "Is that Flint's ship?"

"No, he's dead. But some of his men are here," I answered.

"Not a man with one leg," he cried. "He seemed like such a kind mate; but, oh, he was a bad one."

His story went back to when Flint had taken six men to help him hide the treasure.

"And when he came back, he was by himself. None of us could make out how he did it, six against one," said Ben.

Later, Gunn came back to the island, but he was left there when his sea mates couldn't find the treasure. That was three years ago. We stopped talking when we heard the guns roar.

"Follow me!" I cried, "They have begun to fight!"

Gunn and I ran closer to the beach. Through the trees, we saw a black flag. It was a priate flag. Silver and his men had taken over the ship.

"You know where to find me . . . and come alone," Gunn called, as I went off into the woods

By the time I had found Dr. Livesay and my friends, they had set up a camp. We took turns keeping watch for Silver and his men. I slept through my turn. I woke up when I heard, "Silver's holding up a white flag." (which means he wants the fighting to stop.)

"Stay inside men. Ten-to-one, this is a trick," Captain Smollett said.

Silver had a hard time trying to climb the hill over to our camp. "Don't shoot," he called, as he finally reached the top.

The captain took over and told Silver, "If you have anything to say man, better say it."

"Well Captain," smiled Silver, "we want the treasure and we'll have it. Give us the map and we'll send someone to bring you back home safely. I give you my word."

"Very good. Now hear me. You can't find the treasure and you can't sail the ship without our help. Now, if you come here again, I'll shoot you in the back," finished our ship's captain.

Silver pulled himself up and said with a roar, "Them that die will be the lucky ones!" When he reached the bottom of the hill, the guns went off. His men rushed our camp. When the fighting was over, only the captain was hurt.

THE SURPRISE

COMPREHENSION CHECK

Choose the best answer.

Preview Answer:
b. Jim saw something in the trees.

1. What Jim saw running behind the trees, was
   ___a. Ben Gunn.
   ___b. Flint.
   ___c. a lion.
   ___d. a horse.

2. Ben Gunn told Jim that
   ___a. the island was beautiful.
   ___b. Flint and six men had hidden the treasure on the island.
   ___c. there was no treasure.
   ___d. Silver was a good man.

3. Why did Ben Gunn stay on the island all alone for three years?
   ___a. He thought the island was a nice place.
   ___b. He was tired of working.
   ___c. He wanted to stay on the beach.
   ___d. Silver and his men left him there.

4. While Ben Gunn was telling Jim about the treasure,
   ___a. Silver found them.
   ___b. Dr. Livesay went home.
   ___c. they heard guns roar.
   ___d. someone took their picture.

5. By the time Jim and Ben ran to the beach to see what the fighting was about, they saw a black flag. The flag meant
   ___a. the ship was ready to sail.
   ___b. the weather was going to change.
   ___c. Silver and his men had taken over the ship.
   ___d. all the danger was over.

6. When Silver appeared at Jim's camp holding a white flag,
   ___a. Jim and Silver became friends.
   ___b. Jim and the others knew it was a trick.
   ___c. Jim and the others ran to help him.
   ___d. Jim waved a yellow flag.

7. Silver told Captain Smollett that
   ___a. he and his men wanted the treasure map.
   ___b. he was willing to share the treasure.
   ___c. he didn't want any of the treasure.
   ___d. he and his men had found the treasure.

8. Captain Smollett and his men did not like Long John Silver and his men, because
   ___a. Long John's men had nicer clothes than they did.
   ___b. Silver and his men had lied to them.
   ___c. Silver and his men were smarter than they were.
   ___d. Silver and his men were not friendly.

9. Another name for this story could be
   ___a. "A Walk in the Woods."
   ___b. "Home Again."
   ___c. "The Fighting Begins."
   ___d. "Happy Times."

10. This story is mainly about
    ___a. Silver and his men trying to get the treasure map.
    ___b. Silver and his men looking for food on the island.
    ___c. both groups of men helping each other find the treasure.
    ___d. Silver and his men giving up the fight.

Check your answers with the Comprehension Check Key on page 67.

This page may be reproduced for classroom use.

THE SURPRISE

VOCABULARY CHECK

climb	cried	fight	roar	taken	through

I. Sentences to Finish

Fill in the blank in each sentence with the correct key word from the box above.

1. It is not nice to _____ with one another.

2. "No, you may not go," Dad said with a _____ .

3. Who has _____ my seat?

4. I couldn't see _____ the thick fog.

5. It was hard to _____ to the top of the stairs.

6. She _____ out with joy, "I can't believe I won."

II. Mixed-up Words

First, unscramble the letters in Column A to spell out the key words. Then, match the key words with the right meaning in Column B by drawing a line from the word to the meaning.

Column A

1. drice _____

2. aorr _____

3. ghrotuh _____

4. anket _____

5. mbicl _____

6. thifg _____

Column B

a. to hurt another person

b. shouted out

c. took over

d. to go higher

e. from one side to the other

f. to talk loud

Check your answers with the key on page 70.

MY STORY

PREPARATION

Key Words

cut	(kut)	a deep opening in the skin; to pass across *I cut myself on a piece of glass.*
quickly	(kwik´lē)	moving fast *They ran quickly when they heard the noise.*
rope	(rōp)	a thick string *Mother tied a rope around the dog's neck so he wouldn't run away.*
round	(round)	1. going in a circle *We went round and round the same city street because we were lost.* 2. like a circle *Susan has a round face.*
strange	(strānj)	something you have never seen or heard before; not usual *That was a strange sound that made me jump.*
until	(ən til´)	up to the time of *We stood until the bus came.*

MY STORY

Necessary Words

chance   (chans)   fate; luck; take the risk of; possibility of something happening
We met by <u>chance</u>.

cool   (kül)   more cold than hot
It is a very <u>cool</u> day today.

tip   (tip)   overturn
I bumped into the table and made the glass of milk <u>tip</u>.

MY STORY

The pirate's black flag, the Jolly Roger, was flying.
Silver's men had taken over the Hispaniola. I must get to the ship.

Preview:	1. Read the name of the story.
	2. Look at the picture carefully.
	3. Read the sentences under the picture.
	4. Read the first paragraph of the story.
	5. Then answer the following question.

You learned from your preview that
___ a. no one was hurt in the fight.
___ b. Dr. Livesay was hurt.
___ c. the captain's fighting days were over for a while.
___ d. Silver's men stayed on to help.

Turn to the Comprehension Check on page 40 for the right answer.

Now read the story.

Read to find out what Jim does after the fight.

MY STORY

Silver's men were not to be seen. As for the captain, he had deep cuts and some broken bones. His fighting days were over for a while. We tried to keep him quiet. Dr. Livesay wasn't to be found. We thought he had gone to find Ben Gunn. I was glad he fixed the cut across my hand before he left.

Just thinking about Dr. Livesay walking under the cool trees made me want to leave the hot camp. I put some food into my pockets and took my guns. My idea was to find the white rock, where Ben kept his tiny boat, and set off for a ride. I walked along the beach and saw the ship, with its new flag, rocking on the waves. It was growing dark. I needed to find the boat quickly. I reached the white rock and moved the bushes. There it was, just as Ben told me. It was strange looking and very small -- even for me.

As I climbed into it, I had another strange idea. I would wait until it was very dark. Then I would row over to the Hispaniola. When I had the chance, I would cut her free. She would sail out to sea with Silver's men.

I spent much time going round and round. At last, I made my way over to the ship. I was about to cut the rope, when I came to a full stop. If I cut it all at once, the waves from the large ship might tip over my small boat. I made up my mind to cut the rope, one piece at a time. I lay very quiet and cut and cut until the Hispaniola began to move. The rope began to pass me by in the water. Quickly, I picked it up. I don't know why, but I pulled myself hand over hand until I could touch the ship. I held on to the side. I pulled up to a window just enough to see two men fighting. All at once, I was knocked to the bottom of my boat by a large wave. Next, I heard shouts. The men came running because they knew the ship was moving. I hoped they would not see me. If my tiny boat tipped over, I would be lost at sea. I layed down on the bottom of my boat. I didn't move for hours, as the sea rocked me to sleep.

MY STORY

COMPREHENSION CHECK

Choose the best answer.

1. After the fighting was over, Dr. Livesay was not to be found. His men thought
   ___a. he went home.
   ___b. he was dead.
   ___c. he had gone to find Ben Gunn.
   ___d. he was hiding.

2. Jim also left the camp. He went looking for
   ___a. the tiny boat Ben Gunn had told him about.
   ___b. Silver and his men.
   ___c. Dr. Livesay.
   ___d. a new place to stay.

3. When Jim was walking along the beach looking for the white rock, he saw
   ___a. Dr. Livesay.
   ___b. Ben Gunn.
   ___c. a storm coming up over the mountains.
   ___d. the pirates' flag flying on the Hispaniola.

4. While in the boat, Jim had a strange idea. He decided to
   ___a. row all the way home.
   ___b. look for the treasure himself.
   ___c. sink the Hispaniola.
   ___d. wait till it got dark, and then cut the Hispaniola free.

5. When Jim cut the rope to the Hispaniola,
   ___a. he hoped the ship would sail out to sea with Silver's men.
   ___b. he hoped she would sink.
   ___c. he helped Silver's men set the sails.
   ___d. Jim and his men were on board.

6. Jim did not want his little boat to tip over, so
   ___a. he did not cut the rope.
   ___b. he cut the rope, one piece at a time.
   ___c. he swam out to the Hispaniola.
   ___d. he went and got a bigger boat.

7. With the ship cut free, Jim pulled himself up to a window just enough to
   ___a. jump onto the ship.
   ___b. bang his head and fall into the water.
   ___c. pull his little boat onto the Hispaniola.
   ___d. see two men fighting.

8. If Silver's men knew that Jim was cutting the ship's rope,
   ___a. they would have helped him.
   ___b. they would have asked him why he was doing it.
   ___c. they would have done something terrible to Jim.
   ___d. they would have been very happy.

9. Another name for this story could be
   ___a. "A Walk Along the Beach."
   ___b. "After the Fight."
   ___c. "Round and Round."
   ___d. "Jim's Idea."

10. This story is mainly about
    ___a. Dr. Livesay taking care of Jim.
    ___b. where Ben Gunn kept the boat.
    ___c. Jim trying to get rid of Silver's men.
    ___d. poor Captain Smollett.

Check your answers with the Comprehension Check Key on page 67.

MY STORY

VOCABULARY CHECK

cut	quickly	rope	round	strange	until

I. Sentences to Finish

Fill in the blank in each sentence with the correct key word from the box above.

1. Come _____ or you will miss the train.

2. The baby's face was _____ and fat.

3. Some of the animals at the zoo are very _____ .

4. I _____ my leg while trying to climb the fence.

5. Mom always stays up _____ my brother comes home.

6. I tied a _____ around two trees so I could hang my clothes out to dry.

II. Crossword Puzzle

Use the words from the box above to fill in the puzzle. Use the meanings below to help you choose the right answer.

Down

1. up to the time of
3. thick string
5. moving fast

Across

3. going in circles
4. a deep opening in the skin
6. something you have never seen before

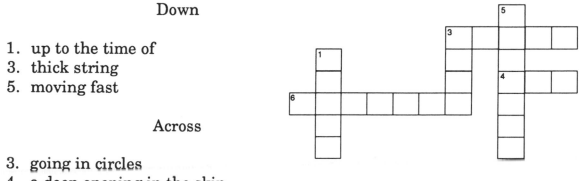

Check your answers with the key on page 70.

ISRAEL HANDS

PREPARATION

Key Words

bottom	(bot´ə m)	the lowest part on which something rests *The kitten hid under the <u>bottom</u> of my chair.*
cap	(kap)	a tight-fitting hat *My <u>cap</u> kept my ears warm.*
hardly	(härd´lē)	not at all; barely *I <u>hardly</u> ate any candy.*
hit	(hit)	to come against someone with a bump *He <u>hit</u> me as he walked by.*
sure	(shu̇r)	certain *She was <u>sure</u> she could do the work.*
throw	(thrō)	to make something move through the air quickly by using your arm *Can you <u>throw</u> the ball fast enough to get him out?*

ISRAEL HANDS

Necessary Words

People

Captain Hawkins   Jim

Israel Hands   a pirate (one of Silver's men) who steers the Hispaniola

ISRAEL HANDS

On the Hispaniola, Jim stood looking around. At first, he did not know what to do.

Preview: 1. Read the name of the story.
2. Look at the picture carefully.
3. Read the sentences under the picture.
4. Read the first paragraph of the story.
5. Then answer the following question.

You learned from your preview that
___ a. Jim was stuck on the Hispaniola.
___ b. Jim could not find the Hispaniola.
___ c. Jim was still on the island.
___ d. Jim did not know how to swim.

Turn to the Comprehension Check on page 46 for the right answer.

Now read the story.

Read to find out about Jim Hawkins and Israel Hands.

ISRAEL HANDS

It became light outside. I woke up to find myself near Treasure Island. The inside of my boat was filled with water, so I used my cap to get most of it out. As the sun grew warmer, I laid my cap out to dry. I looked up as my boat turned. There before me, was the ship again. "Where are the men?" I wondered, as I moved closer and closer. When the boats hit, I jumped onto the side. I felt the water hit the bottom of my feet, so I climbed over to the Hispaniola. My boat had moved away. I was stuck on the Hispaniola with no way to leave.

As I climbed up, I didn't see anyone. The poor ship had been taken apart from top to bottom. Silver's men had been looking for the map. Broken rum bottles were all over. I jumped when I came around the corner and found two men face down. I turned them over. I remembered them fighting the night I cut the rope. One of them was dead. The other man, named Israel Hands, asked me for rum. I gave him a good, long drink. He felt better.

"Well, Mr. Hands," I began, "I've come to take the Hispaniola. Oh yes, I'll take down your black flag and throw it into the sea." I waved my cap and said, "That's the end of Long John Silver and his men."

"I guess you'll want to go to the island, Captain Hawkins," he called.

"Yes, that's a good idea," I answered.

"I'll tell you how to sail her," he said. And in no time at all, we were moving back to Treasure Island.

I believed what I had done was right. I was pleased that I had enough food and water. The only thing that troubled me was the strange, wild look in Israel's eyes every time he smiled at me. We were waiting for a good wind when he said, "My mate is dead. Let's throw him into the sea and be done with it." I knew I wasn't strong enough. I said that it was hardly the kind of job a "captain" should have to do.

"This here's a ship with hardly any luck, Jim. Many a seaman has come and gone," he said.

"I'll take my chances," I answered.

"Look Captain, this rum is making my head hurt. Would you go below and bring me something else to drink?" he asked.

I knew Hands was trying to get me to leave, but I wasn't sure why. The only thing I was sure of was that he was up to no good.

ISRAEL HANDS

COMPREHENSION CHECK

Choose the best answer.

1. The next morning when Jim woke up in his little boat, right before him was
   ___a. the Hispaniola.
   ___b. Dr. Livesay.
   ___c. his mother.
   ___d. Long John Silver.

2. When the boats hit,
   ___a. Jim was thrown into the water.
   ___b. Jim's boat sank.
   ___c. the men came to help him.
   ___d. Jim climbed onto the Hispaniola.

3. The poor ship had been taken apart. Silver's men
   ___a. were having a party.
   ___b. had been looking for the map.
   ___c. were cleaning it up.
   ___d. were angry at Jim.

4. Jim told Israel Hands
   ___a. that he was glad to see him.
   ___b. that he was taking over the Hispaniola.
   ___c. that he needed help cleaning up the ship.
   ___d. that he was sorry to see the black flag being taken down.

5. With Jim as the ship's captain,
   ___a. they sailed home.
   ___b. they sank the ship.
   ___c. they sailed back to Treasure Island.
   ___d. they waited for the others.

6. Even though Israel Hands was helping Jim, Jim
   ___a. wanted to do it all himself.
   ___b. was troubled by the strange look in Israel's eyes.
   ___c. told Israel to leave him alone.
   ___d. was glad they were friends.

7. When Israel asked Jim for something else to drink, Jim knew
   ___a. there was nothing left on the ship.
   ___b. Israel could not still be thirsty.
   ___c. it must be time for lunch.
   ___d. Israel was trying to get him to go below.

8. When Israel Hands said the Hispaniola was an unlucky ship, he meant that
   ___a. the treasure had not been found yet.
   ___b. the ship was sinking.
   ___c. the ship had ghosts on it.
   ___d. many seamen had died on the Hispaniola.

9. Another name for this story could be
   ___a. "On Board the Hispaniola."
   ___b. "Help!"
   ___c. "One Summer Day."
   ___d. "Together Again."

10. This story is mainly about
   ___a. Jim and his friends.
   ___b. Jim taking over the Hispaniola.
   ___c. the pirates' black flag.
   ___d. two men fighting.

Check your answers with the Comprehension Check Key on page 67.

ISRAEL HANDS

VOCABULARY CHECK

bottom	cap	hardly	hit	sure	throw

I. Sentences to Finish

Fill in the blank in each sentence with the correct key word from the box above.

1. I could _____ lift that heavy box.

2. The first time I drove a car, I _____ a fence.

3. I stepped on a pebble and now the _____ of my foot hurts.

4. Let's see who can _____ the ball the fastest.

5. My ears were cold because I did not wear my _____ .

6. Mom was _____ that I would win the race.

II. Word Use

Put a check next to YES if the sentence makes sense. Put a check next to NO if the sentence does not make sense.

1. On the <u>bottom</u> of my head, I wear a hat.   ___ YES ___ NO

2. It was cold outside, so I wore a <u>cap</u> on my hands.   ___ YES ___ NO

3. I <u>hardly</u> had any cookies today.   ___ YES ___ NO

4. John got yelled at because he <u>hit</u> me.   ___ YES ___ NO

5. I was <u>sure</u> that I was right.   ___ YES ___ NO

6. To run fast, you must be able to <u>throw</u>.   ___ YES ___ NO

Check your answers with the key on page 71.

HOW IT HAPPENED

PREPARATION

Key Words

corner	(kôr´nər)	the point where two lines, two walls, etc. meet *He chased me into the <u>corner</u>, and I could not get out.*
piece	(pēs)	one thing; one part of *I had one <u>piece</u> of the pie.*
short	(shôrt)	not long; not tall *The rope was too <u>short</u> to reach the other side of the boat.*
shut	(shut)	close tight; to close by pulling or pushing some part into place *The windows were <u>shut</u> to keep the cold air out.*
small	(smôl)	little; not big; not great *I took a <u>small</u> piece of cake.*
swish	(swish)	to move with a light, brushing sound *His knife went <u>swish</u> as it passed through the air.*

HOW IT HAPPENED

Necessary Words

sand   (sand)   tiny, loose grains of worn-down rock
I went to the beach and got <u>sand</u> in my shoes.

HOW IT HAPPENED

"Israel Hands is up to no good," thought Jim.

Preview:	1. Read the name of the story.
	2. Look at the picture carefully.
	3. Read the sentence under the picture.
	4. Read the first paragraph of the story.
	5. Then answer the following question.

You learned from your preview that
___ a. Israel Hands was a good friend.
___ b. Israel Hands was a clever man.
___ c. Jim Hawkins liked Israel Hands.
___ d. Jim Hawkins gave a knife to Israel Hands.

Turn to the Comprehension Check on page 52 for the right answer.

Now read the story.

Read to find out about the danger that Jim Hawkins is in.

HOW IT HAPPENED

Israel Hands was a clever man. He didn't know I was watching when he pulled himself up. He could hardly stand. His leg hurt, but he moved on his hands and knees enough and found a short knife. He hid it in his small pocket. Then he dropped back to the same spot he was in before.

That's all I needed to know. Hands could move and now he had a knife. Since sailing the Hispaniola would take both of us, I felt I would be safe until we reached the island.

Sailing the big ship was exciting. It was fun watching the ship swish through the sea. I forgot about Hands as I watched and waited for the Hispaniola to hit the sand.

All at once, a strange quiet came over the ship. I turned just in time to see Hands coming at me with the short knife. He had me in the corner. Suddenly, the ship stopped quickly. We fell on top of each other. I jumped up before Hands could get a piece of me. I got out of the corner and climbed as high as I could go.

I pulled out my guns and called, "One more step and I'll blow you to pieces!"

Israel's right hand went back and then I heard something swish through the air. I felt a blow to my arm. Before I knew what happened, my guns went off. Israel Hands fell face first into the water and was now food for the fish. I shut my eyes and shook. It was a good thing, because the knife fell out and I had only a small cut.

I was ready to find my friends again. I hoped Dr. Livesay would not be angry that I left alone. After all, I did bring back the Hispaniola. I tied the ship down safely, then I made my way back to our camp. I could hear the men sleeping as I opened the door. I walked in and stepped on someone. I guessed Mr. Trelawney had shut his eyes and had fallen asleep during his watch. All of a sudden a voice roared, "Who goes there?" It was Silver! There was nothing I could do, as two men jumped on me and held me down to the floor.

HOW IT HAPPENED

COMPREHENSION CHECK

Choose the best answer.

1. Jim saw Israel Hands
   ___a. run around the ship's deck.
   ___b. answer the telephone.
   ___c. hide a knife in his pocket.
   ___d. go for a swim.

2. Jim felt he would be safe
   ___a. with his good friend Israel.
   ___b. until he reached the island.
   ___c. because he could swim.
   ___d. because he was now the captain.

3. First, a strange quiet came over the ship. Then,
   ___a. Jim fell asleep.
   ___b. Israel hid the knife in his pocket.
   ___c. Israel came after Jim with a knife.
   ___d. Israel fell asleep.

4. With Israel Hands after him, Jim
   ___a. pulled out his guns.
   ___b. cried and cried.
   ___c. jumped into the water.
   ___d. took the knife away from Israel.

5. During the fight, Israel fell into the water and
   ___a. Jim jumped in to save him.
   ___b. Jim fell in, too.
   ___c. Jim sailed the ship home.
   ___d. Jim got cut on his arm.

6. Jim was ready to go back to his friends. He hoped
   ___a. Israel could swim.
   ___b. they found the treasure.
   ___c. his mother was home.
   ___d. Dr. Livesay would not be angry with him.

7. First, Jim brought back the Hispaniola. Next, he tied the ship down safely. Then,
   ___a. he went fishing.
   ___b. he made his way back to camp.
   ___c. he took a nap.
   ___d. he went looking for Israel Hands.

8. Jim found that Silver and his men
   ___a. had taken over his old camp.
   ___b. had become good friends.
   ___c. were taking good care of his old camp.
   ___d. were fixing up his old camp.

9. Another name for this story could be
   ___a. "The Picnic."
   ___b. "A Day of Rest."
   ___c. "The Hispaniola."
   ___d. "Dear Mom."

10. This story is mainly about
    ___a. how to fish.
    ___b. how to swim.
    ___c. Jim learning to hunt.
    ___d. Jim bringing the ship back to the island.

Check your answers with the Comprehension Check Key on page 67.

HOW IT HAPPENED

VOCABULARY CHECK

corner	piece	short	shut	small	swish

I. Sentences to Finish

Fill in the blank in each sentence with the correct key word from the box above.

1. I _____ the door on my finger, and it hurt.

2. The teacher made me stand in the _____ because I was talking too much.

3. My friend lives in a _____ house.

4. May I have a _____ of cake?

5. _____ went the arrow as it passed by me.

6. I have only a _____ walk to school.

II. Matching

Write the letter of the correct meaning from Column B next to the key word in Column A.

Column A

1. shut _____

2. corner _____

3. small _____

4. swish _____

5. piece _____

6. short _____

Column B

a. where two walls meet

b. not tall

c. a part of

d. to close tight

e. a light, brushing sound

f. not big

Check your answers with the key on page 71.

SILVER AND ME

PREPARATION

Key Words

count	(kount)	to need someone's help *The team can always <u>count</u> on him to do his best.*
mean	(mēn)	to have in mind *Did you really <u>mean</u> what you said?*
only	(ōn´lē)	and no other *Our dog was the <u>only</u> one with spots.*
sign	(sīn)	a mark, thing, or action, used to point something out or represent something; to write one's name on *A smile is a good <u>sign</u>.*
still	(stil)	staying in the same position; not moving; and yet *I am <u>still</u> here waiting.*
whispered	(hwĭs´- pərd)	spoken softly or very quietly so that no one can hear *She <u>whispered</u> a secret in my ear when no one was looking.*

SILVER AND ME

Necessary Words

fever   (fe - vər)   a higher-than-usual body temperature which means that a person is ill

I had a <u>fever</u> this morning so I stayed in bed all day.

Things

Bible   (biˈbəl)   a book of sacred writings of any religion

The Black Spot   was a page cut out from the Bible and burned black. This page, when given to someone, was believed to cause them bad luck or death.

SILVER AND ME

To my surprise, it was Silver and his men at the camp, not my friends.

Preview: 1. Read the name of the story.
               2. Look at the picture carefully.
               3. Read the sentence under the picture.
               4. Read the first two paragraphs of the story.
               5. Then answer the following question.

You learned from your preview that
___ a. Silver told Jim that Dr. Livesay didn't care about him.
___ b. Silver told Jim that Dr. Livesay was looking for him.
___ c. Jim was glad to see his friends.
___ d. Jim didn't care about Dr. Livesay.

Turn to the Comprehension Check on page 58 for the right answer.

Now read the story.

Read to find out why Jim stays with Silver.

SILVER AND ME

Silver and his men had taken over the camp. There wasn't a sign of my friends. If only I had stayed to help them.

"So, Jim, here you are," said Silver. "I've always liked you. You can't go back to your friends. They don't want you anymore," he said, as he continued to lic. "Dr. Livesay came to us one day, waving the white flag. When we saw the ship was gone, we joined together. He gave us wood. We gave them food. He said they had four men left. They didn't know or care where you were. Are you ready to join us lad?" he asked.

"Join you," I cried, as I wondered about his story. "It was me who heard your plan and told the captain. As for the ship, I have taken her where you'll never find her. Kill me if you like, and I mean it. But I'm the only one who can save your neck when we get home."

Silver's men wanted to kill me right then and there. When they left to have a talk about what to do with me, Silver smiled.

"If you help me when we get back, you can count on me to save you from them pirates as best I can," he said. I knew he was trying to save his own neck, too, so we made a deal.

"Here they come," I whispered.

"Let them come," Silver answered, as his men came back in through the door.

"Step up, lad. Hand over what you have in your hand," said Silver, as he faced his men.

One of the pirates came forward and handed something to Silver. It was a page cut out of a Bible and burned black. It was called the Black Spot, and it meant bad luck for whoever it was given to.

Silver looked the paper over and said, "The Black Spot, well, it don't mean nothing. I'm still your captain."

"Maybe not," cried one of his men. "You let those men go, and you wouldn't let us kill them. Now the ship is gone. And still, there's that boy. We'll hang for sure."

"Is that all?" Silver asked, as he pulled out the treasure map that Dr. Livesay had given him. He threw the map on the floor. The men jumped on it and passed it round and round. Silver had won. They were ready to follow him again.

The next morning I heard Silver say, "We've got a surprise for you, Jim." I looked to see if there was any sign of who was coming around the corner. It was Dr. Livesay. He had a strange look on his face when Silver said, "It's Jim!" The doctor took care of Silver's arm first because they had the fever and, after all, he was a doctor. When he finished, he asked to talk to me. Silver asked me to give my word I wouldn't run for it. I did. He told the doctor how he saved me from the pirates. Then Silver, the doctor, and I walked to the edge of the camp.

"How could you have left us Jim, when the captain was hurt?" asked the doctor.

I didn't mean to, but I began to cry. I told him how Silver had saved me from death and how I had saved the ship.

"The ship! Jim, make a run for it and you're out. Come back with your true friends," the doctor whispered.

"But I told Silver he can count on my word. I can't go with you," I said. I decided to stay with Silver until he found the treasure. That way, I would be safe from Silver's men.

The doctor shook my hand. He told Silver to keep me safe and to be careful when he found the treasure, because Silver's men couldn't be trusted.

SILVER AND ME

COMPREHENSION CHECK

Choose the best answer.

1. Long John Silver wanted Jim to think
    ___a. his friends had left him.
    ___b. he should run away.
    ___c. he could never find the treasure.
    ___d. Silver's men liked him.

2. Silver also told Jim that
    ___a. Dr. Livesay died.
    ___b. Dr. Livesay sailed back home.
    ___c. Dr. Livesay waved the white flag (which means he gave up).
    ___d. Dr. Livesay ran away.

3. Jim told Silver and his men that
    ___a. he had taken the ship where they would never find her.
    ___b. he had the map.
    ___c. he didn't care about Dr. Livesay and his friends.
    ___d. he wanted to go home.

4. When Silver's men left to have a talk about what to do with Jim,
    ___a. Jim ran away.
    ___b. Silver and Jim made a deal to help each other.
    ___c. Silver hid Jim.
    ___d. Jim started to cry.

5. Silver's men were angry at Silver
    ___a. until Silver showed them the treasure map.
    ___b. until Jim yelled at them.
    ___c. until Dr. Livesay had given up.
    ___d. because they wanted Silver to wave the white flag.

6. At the camp one morning, Silver had a surprise for Jim. It was
    ___a. his mother.
    ___b. Israel Hands.
    ___c. Ben Gunn.
    ___d. Dr. Livesay.

7. When Jim and Dr. Livesay talked, Dr. Livesay told Jim
    ___a. he never wanted to see him again.
    ___b. he didn't care where the ship was.
    ___c. to run away from Silver and his men.
    ___d. all hope for finding the treasure was gone.

8. When Jim told Dr. Livesay, "I told Silver he can count on my word," what did he mean?
    ___a. That he and Silver had decided to save each other from harm.
    ___b. Jim knew how to count.
    ___c. Silver knew how to count.
    ___d. Jim didn't mean anything he said.

9. Another name for this story could be
    ___a. "Another Day."
    ___b. "Jim Gives his Word."
    ___c. "More Ideas."
    ___d. "Lost Again."

10. This story is mainly about
    ___a. Dr. Livesay waving the white flag.
    ___b. how the pirates got wood and food.
    ___c. Silver deciding to help Jim.
    ___d. Jim crying to Dr. Livesay.

Check your answers with the Comprehension Check Key on page 67.

SILVER AND ME

VOCABULARY CHECK

count	mean	only	sign	still	whispered

I. Sentences to Finish

Fill in the blank in each sentence with the correct key word from the box above.

1. "What did you _____ by that?" asked John.

2. There was no _____ of the storm before it hit.

3. You can always _____ on me to help out.

4. I was the _____ one to get sick at camp.

5. We were in the library, so we _____ .

6. We have worked so hard, and _____ have more to do.

II. Word Search

All the words from the box above are hidden in the puzzle below. They may be written from left to right or up and down. As you find each word, put a circle around it. One word, that is not a key word, has been done for you.

```
A   R   D   M   S   I   G   N   M
O   J   K   H   C   L   O   E   V
M   E   A   N   O   X   Z   F   B
G   W   O   Q   U   N   K   S   D
S   M   E   P   N   H   S   T   I
H   U   N   M   T   I   D   I   S
U   I   O   N   L   Y   N   L   U
T   V   C   L   B   P   J   L   O
W   H   I   S   P   E   R   E   D
```

Check your answers with the key on page 71.

THE TREASURE

PREPARATION

Key Words

even	(ē´vən)	no matter how unlikely *Even my sister came to the party.*
joke	(jōk)	to make someone laugh from a trick or a story; something funny *Everyone laughed at my joke.*
mind	(mīnd)	not bothered by *I didn't mind telling my story.*
shovel	(shuv´l)	a tool used to dig with *We dug our shovel into the wet dirt.*
suddenly	(sud´n lē)	taking place quickly *The men jumped at us suddenly.*
together	(tə gĕ͞TH´ər)	with each other; at the same time *We walked to school together.*

THE TREASURE

Necessary Words

raised   (rāzd)   moved upward, lifted upward
                                                I <u>raised</u> the blinds so I could see out the window.

THE TREASURE

Although they tried hard to hide it, Silver's men were really afraid.

Preview: 1. Read the name of the story.
                2. Look at the picture carefully.
                3. Read the sentence under the picture.
                4. Read the first paragraph of the story.
                5. Then answer the following question.

You learned from your preview that
___ a. Dr. Livesay told Jim to stay with Silver's men.
___ b. Dr. Livesay told Silver to come with him.
___ c. Dr. Livesay told Silver to be careful if and when he finds the
      treasure.
___ d. Jim told Silver about the treasure.

Turn to the Comprehension Check on page 64 for the right answer.

Now read the story.

Read to find out who finds the treasure.

THE TREASURE

At breakfast, Silver talked about the treasure. Why did Dr. Livesay tell him to be careful when he found it? I couldn't help but wonder why my friends had left our camp.

We took our shovels. We set out to find the treasure. Together, Silver, his men, and I made a long line as we walked across the island. Suddenly, we heard a loud cry at the far end of the line. Everyone ran to see what was wrong. But even Long John Silver stopped short when we found the bones of a dead man. The hands seemed to point the way to the treasure.

"This must be Flint's idea of a joke," said Silver, trying not to look afraid.

"There are six of us. Just like the six men Flint brought here and who never came back. And that's no joke," cried one of Silver's men.

"Come on," Silver called, as he walked alone. The rest of the men stayed close together. As we sat down to rest, Silver looked at the map and pointed to some tall trees.

"There they are," he said, "those are the trees we are looking for."

We were taking out some food, when a voice came singing out from the trees:

FIFTEEN MEN ON A DEAD MEN'S CHEST

YO HO HO AND A BOTTLE OF RUM.

"It's Flint!" roared one man suddenly, and he ran off into the bushes. The others were too afraid to move. Silver stood up and called, "I'm here to get the treasure. You can count on that. I wasn't afraid of Flint even when he was living and I'm . . . I'm not afraid of him now that he's dead. Come to think of it men, that voice didn't sound like Flint. Why, it sounded more like . . . like . . . Ben Gunn." The men began to laugh.

"Nobody minds old Ben Gunn whether he's living or not," said one man.

We started out again. When we had just about ten yards to go, we saw something. Silver hopped to the spot as fast as he could. He shook as he roared, "Someone's been here and there's nothing left in the bottom of this hole." The men couldn't believe this. They dropped their shovels, jumped in the hole, and dug like animals with their hands. They knew they had been tricked and they were angry with Long John.

"Jim," Silver whispered, "get your guns ready. There's going to be trouble."

The men raised their arms and came at us. Just in time, guns fired out from the bushes. When it was over, Ben Gunn and Dr. Livesay had saved Silver and me. (I knew the only reason they saved Silver was because he had saved me from his own men.)

We walked back to the ship. Dr. Livesay told us how Ben had taken the treasure to his cave. That is why the doctor had moved his men from the camp to the cave, to watch the treasure. This way, too, they wouldn't catch the fever that Silver's men had, back at the wet camp. It took us days to count the money. Then we put it into bags and set sail for home. While at sea, Ben came running to us with a secret he couldn't wait to tell. He had helped Long John Silver get away in a small boat. We ran to the treasure . . . there was only one bag missing. We were glad to be rid of Silver, so the one bag was worth it!

That's the end of my story that happened long ago, and that was the last time I ever saw or heard of Long John Silver. And while I don't mind telling my story, I will never set sail or go back to Treasure Island again.

THE TREASURE

COMPREHENSION CHECK

Choose the best answer.

1. When the men were out with their shovels looking for the treasure, they heard a loud cry. One of the men had found
    ___a. a beautiful bird.
    ___b. the bones of a dead man.
    ___c. the treasure chest.
    ___d. the Hispaniola.

2. Silver said that what they found was
    ___a. Flint's idea of a joke.
    ___b. very silly.
    ___c. really terrible.
    ___d. something to worry about.

3. The men were afraid, so they stayed close together. They were just about to eat, when
    ___a. it started to rain.
    ___b. the fire went out.
    ___c. it was time to go home.
    ___d. a voice came singing out from the trees.

4. The men were sure what they heard was Flint, a dead man. What they really heard was
    ___a. the ship's bells.
    ___b. a monkey.
    ___c. Ben Gunn.
    ___d. a bird.

5. When Silver and his men found the spot where the treasure was buried,
    ___a. they found the chest.
    ___b. they found fifteen men.
    ___c. they found many animals.
    ___d. they found that someone had already taken the treasure.

6. The pirates thought that Silver and Jim had tricked them. The pirates were about to go after them when, just in time,
    ___a. the police came.
    ___b. Jim and Silver ran.
    ___c. Ben Gunn and Dr. Livesay saved them.
    ___d. Jim and Silver swam out to the Hispaniola.

7. Who had the treasure?
    ___a. Ben Gunn
    ___b. Jim's mother
    ___c. Long John Silver
    ___d. Israel Hands

8. Ben Gunn probably helped Silver get away because
    ___a. Silver gave him money.
    ___b. Silver wanted to go home on his own.
    ___c. Ben Gunn did not trust Silver.
    ___d. Ben Gunn wanted the treasure for himself.

9. Another name for this story could be
    ___a. "Ben Gunn and the Chest."
    ___b. "Silver's Men."
    ___c. "The Cave."
    ___d. "No Treasure."

10. This story is mainly about
    ___a. what happened to the treasure.
    ___b. what happened to the Hispaniola.
    ___c. what happened to Silver.
    ___d. what happened on the way back home.

Check your answers with the Comprehension Check Key on page 67.

THE TREASURE

VOCABULARY CHECK

even	joke	mind	shovel	suddenly	together

I. Sentences to Finish

Fill in the blank in each sentence with the correct key word from the box above.

1. I wanted to make her laugh, so I told her a _____ .

2. The teacher doesn't _____ if you ask him for help.

3. I have my _____ and my seeds, and now I am ready to plant.

4. _____ , the lights went out.

5. As long as we are _____ , I will not be alone.

6. We were told that _____ little children could come to the party.

II. Mixed-Up Words

First, unscramble the letters in Column A to spell out the key words. Then, match the key words with the right meaning in Column B by drawing a line from the word to the meaning.

Column A

1. hovels _____

2. snuldedy _____

3. koje _____

4. dimn _____

5. thegoret _____

6. neev _____

Column B

a. with each other

b. not bothered by

c. no matter how unlikely

d. a tool used for digging

e. something funny

f. taking place quickly

Check your answers with the key on page 72.

This page may be reproduced for classroom use.

NOTES

COMPREHENSION CHECK ANSWER KEY
Lessons CTR-B-31 to CTR-B-40

LESSON NUMBER	QUESTION NUMBER										PAGE NUMBER
	1	2	3	4	5	6	7	8	9	10	
CTR-B-31	b	c	a	d	a	b	a	ⓑ	△d	[d]	10
CTR-B-32	b	a	ⓓ	c	c	b	a	b	△d	[a]	16
CTR-B-33	b	a	a	d	b	c	a	ⓐ	△b	[c]	22
CTR-B-34	d	a	b	d	b	a	c	ⓑ	△a	[c]	28
CTR-B-35	a	b	d	c	c	b	a	ⓑ	△c	[a]	34
CTR-B-36	c	a	d	d	a	b	d	ⓒ	△d	[c]	40
CTR-B-37	a	d	b	b	c	b	d	ⓓ	△a	[b]	46
CTR-B-38	c	b	c	a	d	d	b	ⓐ	△c	[d]	52
CTR-B-39	a	c	a	b	a	d	c	ⓐ	△b	[c]	58
CTR-B-40	b	a	d	c	d	c	a	ⓒ	△a	[a]	64

○ = Inference (not said straight out, but you know from what is said)

△ = Another name for the story

☐ = Main idea of the story

NOTES

VOCABULARY CHECK ANSWER KEY

Lessons CTR B-31 to CTR B-40

LESSON
NUMBER

PAGE
NUMBER

31   THE CAPTAIN'S STORY   11

I. 1. sea
    2. stories
    3. leg
    4. watch
    5. ago
    6. terrible

II.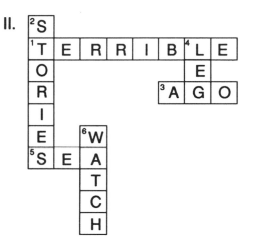

32   GETTING READY   17

I. 1. eyes
    2. myself
    3. wild
    4. answered
    5. shook
    6. quiet

II. 1. NO
    2. YES
    3. YES
    4. NO
    5. YES
    6. NO

33   SETTING SAIL   23

I. 1. secret
    2. exciting
    3. careful
    4. angry
    5. remember
    6. wonder

II. 1. c
    2. d
    3. e
    4. f
    5. b
    6. a

VOCABULARY CHECK ANSWER KEY

Lessons CTR B-31 to CTR B-40

LESSON NUMBER		PAGE NUMBER

34   TROUBLE ON THE SHIP   29

I. 1. join
   2. might
   3. ahead
   4. kill
   5. clever
   6. believe

II.

```
W  B   N   J  O  I  N   A
J  E   Z   X  Q  B  C   H
   K   L   N  R  T  D  F   E
   I   I   M  I  G  H  T   A
   L   E   V  R  O  M  S   D
   L   V   C  L  E  V  E  R
P  E   K   T  U  W  X   Z
O  Q   S   A  P  P  L   E
```

35   THE SURPRISE   35

I. 1. fight
   2. roar
   3. taken
   4. through
   5. climb
   6. cried

II. 1. cried, b
   2. roar, f
   3. through, e
   4. taken, c
   5. climb, d
   6. fight, a

36   MY STORY   41

I. 1. quickly
   2. round, round
   3. strange
   4. cut
   5. until
   6. rope

II.

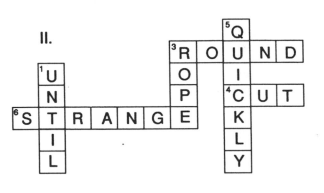

VOCABULARY CHECK ANSWER KEY

Lessons CTR B-31 to CTR B-40

LESSON
NUMBER

PAGE
NUMBER

37   ISRAEL HANDS   47

I.
1. hardly
2. hit
3. bottom
4. throw
5. cap
6. sure

II.
1. NO
2. NO
3. YES
4. YES
5. YES
6. NO

38   HOW IT HAPPENED   53

I.
1. shut
2. corner
3. small
4. piece
5. Swish
6. short

II.
1. d
2. a
3. f
4. e
5. c
6. b

39   SILVER AND ME   59

I.
1. mean
2. sign
3. count
4. only
5. whispered
6. still

II.

```
A  R  D  M (S  I  G  N) M
O  J  K  H (C  L  O  E  V
(M  E  A  N) O  X  Z  F  B
G  W  O  Q  U  N  K (S  D
S  M  E  P  N  H  S  T  I
H  U  N  M (T  I  D  I  S
U  I (O  N  L  Y) N  L  U
T  V  C  L  B  P  J  L  O
(W  H  I  S  P  E  R  E  D)
```

VOCABULARY CHECK ANSWER KEY

Lessons CTR B-31 to CTR B-40

LESSON NUMBER		PAGE NUMBER
40 THE TREASURE		65

I.
1. joke
2. mind
3. shovel
4. Suddenly
5. together
6. even

II.
1. shovel, d
2. suddenly, f
3. joke, e
4. mind, b
5. together, a
6. even, c